Ripples

Collection of simple, elegant and meditative poems

Subhash Chandra Gupta

Qurate
quratebooks.com

RIPPLES

Collections of simple, elegant and meditative poems

Subhash Chandra Gupta

Published in 2024

© Published by

qurate
quratebooks.com

Qurate Books Pvt. Ltd.

Goa 403523, India

www.quratebooks.com

Tel: 1800-210-6527, Email: info@quratebooks.com

ISBN: 978-93-58983-55-5

Dedicated to

My late Mother and Father

Foreword

Writing a book is not an easy task for any individual. Composing poems is actually very challenging for a person who is not a professional writer. It can be possible only when a person keep on writing for a long period of time till he see that a substantial number of composition had been completed. Similarly, I got involved in writing poems as expressing my feelings through poems becomes my hobby as an amateur writer. Hope this will be appreciated by readers. It is very important for a new writer/Author to be encouraged.

Preface

The power and beauty of poem is it's brevity, simplicity, topicalness and thoughtfulness.

Methodically, "Ripples" encompasses topics like; Social, Economic, Cultural and Political matters. Apart from this, it also touches some aspects of personal memories related to childhood, school days.

Besides, it also includes sketches of important historical and contemprorary leaders.

Along with this, author has tried to explain some familiar valuable words, and topics of personal interest, hobbies etc.

The purpose of writing poems is to convey my thoughts and feelings with the help of few words and in more effective way than in any other form of literary style.

The book is divided into different sections to suit the taste of readers of various tastes. I have given importance to short poems in place of long ones. This is only because to save the time of readers and making more graspable and enjoyable to them. I wish that readers will welcome my first endeavour (book) and neglect any shortcoming they find.

I even wish to achieve name and fame in this field and become a professional writer.

I am publishing my book under the banner of Qurate Books Pvt. Ltd. which is committed to support, help and boost the moral of new writers. I am very much hopeful that through the efforts of my publishers my book reaches in the hands of maximum number of book lovers and I get recoganised in this prestigious field.

Last but not the least, although the title of my book is "Ripples" but my objective of writing is to make it a big WAVE among the brave heart of it's readers.

Acknowledgement

The book "Ripples" is collection of poems written by me with great pain as it wasn't easy to write my feelings and thought at one stroke. It has become possible only with my efforts in last ten- fifteen years.

At first, I thank almighty God, with the blessings of whom I am able to put together my diverse compositions in sufficient number that has made possible to plan myself to bring these together before everyone, in the form of a book.

I would like to thank my sincere friends, Facebook friends, relatives and well-wishers whose necessary moral boosting approach have given me unseen strength to pursue my efforts with desirable interest.

I am consciously and unconsciously indebted to my survey of poems in books, newspapers and magazines' that made me wonder, amused and curious about this form of writing.

I specially acknowledge the very maturity of my ideas in my whole academic career which provided me accumulated knowledge on various themes and issue.

I thank my elder son (Rahul) who helped a lot at the time of typing my manuscript specially in preparing pdf of it, from his personal Lap top. Even I am thankful to my wife (Punam), my daughter (Deeksha) and my younger son (Anay), who all always kept bothered about the finishing of my book.

I sincerely thank my publisher, advisor, supervisor, under the keen interest and guidance of whom the project of my first book has been completed.

Contents

Chapter II : My Social life 29-74

Introduction

The book "Ripples" (a collection of poems) has touched several aspects of life which are relevant or concerning to most of the common people of our country. The view of Author is although personal but it has also universal character. The feelings, emotions, thoughts and actions are particular as much as general in nature. I have remained honest in highlighting many truths related to me and the society to which I am a part. The book provide me to explore some important events of my personal life and also social and political realities. I hope the book will not only do entertainment to it's readers but also bring before them a new vista and perspective about an individual's life and society as a whole. Poetry gives us chance to express ourselves in few words. The poems are written in conventional and non conventional style (e.g; Haikus).

Chapter - I

My Personal Life

The Holy River Ganga

O' the holy river Ganges
Flowing from Gangotri
to Gangasagar, meant for
holy dip for hermit and sages,
provided location for pilgrim cities
and attracts many praises
by common folk,
for it's purity and sacredness
from ancient ages.

Great civilizations grew
on it's Bank and nourished,
at the lap of river Ganga
and it's vast fertile plain,
yielded variety of food crops ,
made the plain 'a land of riches'.

In the recent times,
the pollution of river Ganga
is alarming and suggest
the failings; in our responsibility

and the eroding of
common people's reverence.
The failure to clean river Ganga poses
severe consequence!

If we don't follow,
the Ganga action plan,
it will endanger,
future generation's life.
Let's take pledge,
for safe drinking water,
what the common man,
look and wish to strive.

Moreover, we shouldn't
make any compromises,
in checking the diminishing
numbers of Gangetic whale.
A special measure is needed
for retrieving their life,
so that, all kinds of negativity,
we must dispell.

The course of river Ganga

Down from the mountain slopes,
And the ravine valley,
Upto the foot hill,
The Ganga water run vigorously,
Becomes broad and tranquil,
When touches the plain earth,
During the flood season,
Enrages the water waves frequently.
Carry away the lives of
Human, cattle and destroying
The precious crops.
Food crisis becomes likely.

Government undertake survey
To provide relief wisely and quickly.

I dreamt a dream

Once I dreamt a dream,
It was sunny dream!
It was like a day dream,
Real and clear dream!

Dream was evident and real,
It was vivacious and believable,
Dream was seen and enjoyable,
It was ofcourse a dream not real.

Dream was sweet but made me sad!
Dream was blind, blunt and bad!
Dream was awesome but I was ignorant!
Dream was not blessing but tyrant!

The fortune of future vs The future of fortune

Future is stored in the womb of present.
fortune is determined by the deeds of man.
fortune is fixed, though it can be forged.
fortune sail and propel according to our wishes.
Even fortune will disclose the future of man.
The Man and the Nature will shape the fortune of future.

Wonder the world of Flowers

O' Wonder the world of flowers,
your fragrance,makes us crazy.
Your spectrum of colours,
makes our surrounding charming.
You blossom,
to Spread smiles everywhere .
You dance ,
with the blowing breeze.
Bees and butterflies,
hovers for your sweet nectar.
The gardener,
plucks you for making garland.
The worshippers,
carry you for religious rituals.

The decorators,
make use in marriage parties.
The flowers are gift of Nature,
we give flowers as a gift to our teachers.
The juice of some flowers,
used for making ointment and squash.
We do gardening of flowers,
for pleasure and cash.

Wonder that was India

India, one of the oldest
ancient river valley civilization,
became the forerunner of
present Urban civilization.
Takshila and Nalanda University
rose as center of Education
The arrival of Aryans led to
the rise of Vedic civilization.
The four 'Vedas' are
the oldest literary composition.
Indian clothes and spices were
imported in the western world,
In the field of metallurgy,
India was wizard in the world.

The religious and secular texts
were written in profuse number.
Vedic, Buddhist and Jain philosophy,
Influenced ancient Indian culture.
The Maurya and Gupta rulers were
great statesman and emperors .

They were great conquerors,
Who also defeated foreign invaders.
Patronized art and architecture,
Proved themselves as great builders.
Panini, patanjali kautilya, and kalidasa
became famous literary scholars.
Aryabhatt, Varahmira, Bishnugupta were
great mathematician and astronomers.

Memories

Some memories are 'extinct',
because they are not distinct.

Some memories are 'dormant',
Time to time become vehement.

Some memories are 'active',
as they are eternal and creative.

Memory take us in the past
Good memory always last.

Memory make everyone smile
On their silly mistakes and action futile.

Monsoon Vibes

Monsoon is a season,
Rain rain every region.
Monsoon is a seasonal wind,
Boon for the farmers of Hind.

It give us relief from summer season,
Everyone welcome it for this reason.
Monsoon clouds carry plenty of rain,
makes people worry again and again.

Monsoon cloudy weather facinates everyone,
Our surrounding becomes cool and winsome.
Monsoon clouds hide Sun for several days,
Persistent rain disrupts our life in many ways.

Outing require shoes, umbrella or raincoat,
Flood water, in many towns, requires lifeboat.
Monsoon becomes rejoicing with snacks and sauce,
Intermittent picturesque rain gives us required pause..

Faith vs Truth

We all worship God,
But, no one has seen him.

We talk about ALIENS,
But, no one has witnessed them.

We fear of SPIRITS,
Although, no one has seen them.

We hear of UFO,
Although, no one has observe it .

We read about SWARG and NARAK,
But, we have Idea, only a little bit .

Faith is our blind trust
Truth is also sometimes we don't trust.

Faith is imposed from outside,
Truth is which exists and reside.

Life

Life is struggle and struggle is life,
In every sphere of life we see struggle,
as it is always present in the
individual, social economic or political life,

We shall not give up struggle in our life,
Life of great men always remained in struggle,
Their life still stands inspiring for us,
So struggle, to keep alive struggle, in our life.

My School

My school is a famous school,
very lovely and dearest,
to my friends and me,
Heaven of education for many!
My School imbibe
simple and great thoughts;
adhere old and new
principles and precepts!
To make clear
each and every subject,
the school follow broader
understanding and concept!

To impart everyone,
clear and deep knowledge,
my school has a mission,
with such a distinct vision.
Quality education is ultimate and final,
whether it is textual or vocational .

Happy Teacher's Day

Every year teacher and students,
Celebrate teacher's day.
Teachers are the noble creatures,
Show students rightful way.
Teacher is source of infinite knowledge,
glitters the world with perennial rays.
Teachers are like streams of water,
keeps on moving, nowhere stay.
Teachers are like architects who,
make us happy and gay.
Teachers are honoured and respeced,
However, many get only a meagre pay.
Teachers are exploited and neglected,
a harsh truth everyone say.

Children's Day

Happy children's day,
Hello! What do you say.
Enjoyment and cheerful day,
Wish you goodness all the way.

Do your study and play,
Time passes only deeds stay.
Be moral! Everyone say,
Be humane, all of us pray

Christmas Day

Christmas day,
A very pious day.
This is; I say
And everyone say.
This is a day
Which show us Right way
This is the day
For Christ we pray
This is the day
When all are happy gay
Christmas day
Let violence go and peace stay .

Act of pondering

At times, something sprout
In my thought
It is always painstaking
What I cought
After a battle, somehow
I myself thought
To overcome my weakness
With courage I fought.
The idea which I sighted
slowly slowly silently shout
When I noticed something
I want to discover to aught
Always I have to dicipher
To make it clear to taught.

Gardening

Gardening is a good exercise.
It is a wise advise.
At the sunset and sunrise,
Lovely flowers make us mesmerize.

Everyone must nurture and save plants!
Plants are environment 'purifying plants'.
Some plants bear fruits and some simply flowers,
Plant's woods are used as fuel and making furnitures,
Planting new plants increase our forest areas.

Gardening and horticulture are done in urban areas.
For some it is Past time and for some creative job.
It keeps us busy, healthy and really a pleasure rob.
kitchen garden, raised in front of a house or backyard,
make the house beautiful, elegant with sward.

Destiny

Who fixes destiny
of a man?
Whether it's God or Karma
of a man!

We all wants to reach
our destination,
Whether it is
Temporal or Spiritual.

We can achieve these,
with our determination.
To attain NIRWANA,
the aim is final.

We should think about
Our destiny
But More elieve on making our
Own destiny.

Morals

Early to bed early to rise,
This is the maxim of wise,
This is not a bad advise.
Follow this to make the life nice.

Never do physical fight,
Neither engage in verbal bite,
Love and peace make the life bright,
Good morals we must highlight.

Today surf on Ripples,
Tomorrow ride on waves,
Make life like high tides and tsunami waves.
Let not anti social elements escape.

Truth

Truth always triumph,
Truth must triumph.
Truth should prevail everywhere,
Truth has moral Power.
Truth clean our soul,
Truth is beautiful.
Always speak truth,
Work for truth.
Live a truthful life,
Only truth will remain alive.

Comparing Science, Philosophy and History

Science is based on the observation of
Known and unknown physical thing or phenomena.
Philosophy is based on the imagination of
Unknown Ideal social system i.e; unreal.
History is based on the observation of
Written knowledge about physical or social world.
History is sometimes Philosophy,
and sometimes Science.
Science is to a large extent objective.
Whereas, History is for some objective,
and for others Subjective.

Father's Day

(An Ideal Father)

I am grateful to almighty father!
Also my mundane father!
Who gave me power to struggle,
Courage to overcome any hurdle,
Whether natural or supernatural,
Either fancy or actual.
As a father, I am very humble,
Never imposing and ready to mingle.
Allow my offsprings required Liberty,
To get success and achieve prosperity.
Father is the pivot of the family,
He is the kalptaru of his family.
Father is the final hope and treasure Island,
Where children anchor their emergency fund.
No body can take the place of a father,
As he is the family gardener and it's well-wisher.

Chapter - II

My Social Feelings

Memory Bank

(Past through the eyes of present)

As I pass through,
my memory tunnel,
idea appear crude and rough,
then it filters through the memory funnel.

Mind acts as a binocular,
searching something spectacular,
Memory is like a building block,
Past surfaces when we give a knock.

Memory is always about outstanding thing,
It bounce up when we purposely think.
Memories make many deeply sink and swim,
in the pond of memory spring.

New year's thinking

New year is approaching!
New hopes are emerging!
All are praying,
All are singing,
All are cheering,
All are chatting,
Some are shouting,
Few are whispering,
None is pondering,
Some look for discovering,
A tint of hope for inventing.

A New year is knocking !
New desires are surfacing!!
Everyone is wishing,
What he is missing.
Many needs are rising,
Many tasks are awaiting,

Many plans are upcoming,
Some are really promising,
Others are depressing,
Mission on for conquering,
Nothing left for lingering,

A New year is beginning !
New efforts are emerging!!

Sun-1

From dawn to dusk time,
We get plenty of sunshine,
We do work in the daytime,
Evening to night is rest time.

Sun is like a fire ball,
Which will never fall !
Sunrays spread with the sunrise,
We awake with birds chirping noise!

We desire our son like Sun,
Their names must glow as solar flare!
Life seems the gift of Sun,
Sun is supreme, we must declare !

Sun thou the source of life,
Sun thou the sign of power,
Sun thou the form of God,
Sun thou the pivot of world.

Wise thought

(On the issue of development)

The tasks of the development of
our country, society or an individual
are not fulfilled hitherto.

Independence,Green revolution and
Industrialisation have resulted in
limited and lopsided development too.

Narrow and selfish thinking,
make the development process prolong.
Both Inefficiency and corruption,
hindering the development so long.

Without the perspective of
Nationalism, humanism and democracy,
the development will not be real,
although it could be only partial.

Spring

Something comes in my mind and keep echoing,
Oh! It's nothing but onset of lovely Spring,
Birds begin singing, new leaves look smiling,
The cool blowing wind make us feel like king.

Something comes in my mind and keep echoing,
Oh! I am sure it's onset of pleasant monsoon,
Sky is filled by clouds which rain now and then,
Give relief from summer heat and fruits to eat.

Often something knocking at the door!
Sometimes it's likely my over expenses,
Which may bring financial hardships in future.
Often something knocking at the door!

Sometimes passivism and sometimes optimism,
At times, we loose and the other time we win.
The truth is,life is full of ups and down,
So, always keep in mind this vision.

Search

A search,
Long before our independence,
tradition and modernity were
two pillars of our Political salvation,
to make India an Independent Nation.

A research about,
the Leaders of Independent country,
who forgot their old golden memory,
followed Globalization and Westernization,
to spearhead economic and social Revolution.

India is no more inward looking,
Embracing exotic and welcoming them,
Tendency is now of outward looking,
Showing likeness and forthcoming to them.

Globalization is changing the world into a village.
Will it change the conditions of Indian village?
There is the rise of new corporate culture.
But it has overshadowed the Indian culture.

Nature Speaks

Moon, Sun and Stars,
They are very far.
Solid, liquid and Gas,
Earth has lovely face.

Plateaus, Hills and Mountains,
Sources of rivers and fountains.
Rivers, Oceans and Lakes,
Humans have many stakes.

Deserts, Plateaus and Plains,
They are connected by Trains.
Trees, Plants, Grass, Herbs and Shurbs,
Provide vegetables fruits and flowers.

Dream

Dream is when dreamt,
get potray on the screen.
Dream is sometimes dreamt,
to get materialize to be seen.

Dreams are sometimes personal,
Dreams are sometimes social,
Dreams are sometimes National,
Dreams are sometimes International.

Dreams are sometimes horrible,
Dreams are sometimes enjoyable,
Dreams are sometimes emotional,
Dreams are sometimes special.

Dreams are often mysterious,
Which have actually no roots.
Dreams are often suspicious,
Which have so many shoots.

Dreams are mainly 'night dreams'
As man dreams unconsciously.
Dreams are also 'Day Dreams',
As man is dreaming consciously.

Dreams are half truth, half false,
Morning dreams are never false,
Dreams are often forgettable,
All dreams are not realisable .

Dream may be small,
Dreams may be big,
Dreams may be altruistic,
Dreams may be realistic.

Everything is well and fine,
When dreams comes true,
Wait for the favourable time,
When dreams becomes true.

All know and talk about dream,
'Reality bites' and so fall in dream.
Many lives in the realm of dream,
We,translates a few of our dream.

Society x- rayed

I tends to draw the picture of society.
It may be consciously or in anxiety.

There is great loss of goodness from our society.
Also, banishment of our faith on heavenly diety.
So is, eloping of liberal thought and law of piety.
Further, there is gradual fading of human entity.
Alarming is the passive thinking in the society!

Actually, man is facing problems in great variety.
Some are human created and some by Almighty!
Live well or live with problems, let's fix our priority!
Salvation lies in proximity with truth and divinity!
Work to explore and establish the world of gaiety.

I tend to draw the picture of society.
It may be consciously or in anxiety.

Adversity never comes alone

Our country is facing
the chronic problem
of backwardness,
a legacy of past,
and a fact of present.
In the era of globalisation,
the nature of
development is awesome.

There are more
instances of failures,
than the successes.
We are trying our best,
to make our economy
Independent and self reliant,
but instead it's dependency
on foreign countries has
also alarmingly increased,

due to dearth of capital,
and the need of advance
technology and war weapons,
for security reasons.

The surging unemployment
in the poverty ridden society
has developed undesirable
anxiety and acts as
a threat for social amity.

Border disputes, religious terrorism,
along with the occurrences of
different forms of natural disaster,
making impossible
the economic growth faster.

The eruption of
notorious disease like Corona,
make us bewilder about
the fate of
human lives and livelihood of
millions of people in the country
and all over the world.

It seems that the restoration of
the world economy
will not be easier and faster,
as the economic recession
is bound to long last,
due to the policy of
social distancing and isolation.

The revival of economic
and other activities
will not be in desired proportion.

The agenda 21
of the Earth summit,
to fight the global problems like
World terrorism,
Environmental deterioration,
Hunger and poverty,
Human right violation,
is at present overshadowed
by the growth of Corona threat.

Match of the world

The World is spiraling ahead,
surmounting several loggerheads.
The irony is that man makes his destiny,
Sometimes bleak and sometimes shiny.

Normally Man makes the nature productive,
but often his neglect makes it destructive.
The man has forged society,developed culture,
glorious civilizations and outerspace adventure.

Still many problems before the man is persisting,
Particularly, economic conditions are disturbing.
Hunger for Industrial growth makes the man err,
and the greed of few,have made all of us suffer.

The philanthropic and cooperative attitude,
can become saviour of millions of destitute.
All the time of distress,we must shape our doom,
Any greed and neglect will make our life gloom.

Sun-2

Earth, revolve around the Sun ,
In 365 days,complete revolution one.
Winter, Spring, Summer and Autumn,
These seasons occur one by one.

Sun bestows us Life and Light,
Sun give us Energy and Heat,
Sun is our Star in the sky,
Sun is afar, too far to fly,

Sun causes summer rain ,
Help farmers grow grain.
Sun rises in the east,
Sun Sets in the west.

Sun is very huge and hot,
We call it our Sun god.
Man always prays him a lot,
We expects everytime his nod.

Happy New Year

Happy new year!
Hello! everybody dear.
Think no tear,
Keep aside fear,
Make everyone cheer,
Simple and be clear.

Happy new year!
At the outset of every year,
To make all steer,
Through out the year.
Celebration for a new year,
Make grand welcome with cheer.

Journey (Past and Present)

In the antiquity,
the journey of man
was not easy and safe,
But due to nomadic life
People used to travel continuously
From one place to another
In search of food water and shelter.

After the advent of agriculture,
Man started sedentary life,
but the surplus grain production
forced them to travel far and wide.
When the Metal Age arrived,
Production of new goods thrived,
with the growth of ancient civilization,
Journey of man move ahead
For educational and religious mission.

In the medieval times,
in the search of Eldorado
led to geographical discoveries.

Adventurous sea voyages began,
for the sake of greed and glory.

In the modern period,
due to industrial revolution,
mass production of goods started
by the European countries.
Trading companies travelled
different parts of the world,
to buy and sell their goods
for profit and bullion accumulation.
To make control over market,
they began the process of colonization.

In the twentieth century,
started the process of recolonization,
that led to the rise of Independent nation.
In the post world wars scenario,
trade boomed due to the need of
war reconstruction and modernization.
The development of telecommunication
and advanced means of transportation,
encourage even common people,
to travel across the world,
to discover world culture and civilization.

In the Twenty first century,
new avenues for travel led to the rise of
tourism and hospitality Sector.
The movement of goods and people
are on the tremendous rise,
due to satellite communication
Meant to provide vast information,
in the period of globalisation.

Life Rebinds

Year after year,
we have reached so far.
Past and memories,
shining like twinkling stars.

Past is bitter, Past is sweet,
Memories always fly and tweet.
As,we become sad or happy,
mind discover memory floppy.

Recall! man lives not in years,
but in extraordinary deeds.
It convey, one and all 'dears',
to follow good deeds.

Friends and Friendship

Friends are friends, as they don't care,
Caste, creed, class and culture of others.
Friends are pastime brothers or sisters,
to care and share all kinds of emotions;
Be it sorrow, happiness, failure or success.
Some friends are surely forgettable,
Some friends are actually memorable.
Friends are everywhere, but know the best,
Who rest in our soul and passes every test.
Friends and Friendship are alive on the Earth,
As, a few good friends take the credit they worth.

Flood

Oh flood, don't become deluge!
Don't make modern man confuse!
In the past flood caused destruction in profuse.
Some rivers were known for their curse,
Unless tamed the situation will remain worse.
Oh flood! We have a humble urge,
Don't show your barbaric gurge,
Don't allow water to highly surge,
Let not again human settlements submerge,
Ancient Harappa rebuilt after each seven submerge.

Choice of Environment

Try to fit ourselves,
in a given environment.
Man live in hot, wet cool,
as well as snowy environment.
Man is capable to adapt in,
all types of environment.
If not, select one which is
one's favourite environment.
Man is also capable of creating,
artificial and cozy environment.
The objective is to establish,
a sustainable environment.

Jalebi – The National Sweet

O wonderful spiral sweet,
You are my national sweet.
I wish always to eat and eat,
I want always to treat and treat.

I pray to diety and beg please!
Make the world, free of disease,
so that we always feel at ease,
Have mouthful sweet and no excuse.

Please, please, please!!

Festivals

We celebrate religious festivals
Through out the year
We observe cultural festivals
to make society steer
We admire national festivals
With admiration and cheer

Of all the Indian festivals
Religious festivals influence us the most
Hindus celebrate religious festivals
In which the devotion of poor is utmost

Book fair, Crafts mela,Trade fairs
are modern emerging Yearly festivals
Popularity of such trending events
Could ensure business upheavals.

Modern Life

There is sea change
in modern life.
Individualism and sound
financial status are
essential for a prosperous life.
Lust of money and power,
for a small group of people,
fail to breach the social strife.
Growth of power blocks
and money magnets,
make the country neglect,
its economy to thrive.
Materialism has given rise,
to sophisticated, technological
and luxurious life.

Good Morning

We say Good morning,
to each other.
Because we pass greeting
to whom we bother.
At the first morning meeting,
make us to utter.
We start our chatting,
to impress other.
As we go for Facebook surfing,
we find all well wishers.
Competing in WhatsApp messaging,
as we open it's shutter.
Ofcourse no harm in saying good morning,
to our friends and well wisher.
This greeting makes our face smiling,
and bring smile at the face of others.

Manifestation of Rain

Rain is very fascinating
Often comes with rythmic singing
Sometimes it is very heartening
Sometimes tends to threatening.

Sometimes,it is raining cats and dog.
In winter, it brings lots of fog.
Rain is sometimes drizzling rain
Rain is sometimes, heavy rain.

Rain is cyclonic
Rain is stormy
Rain is natural
Rain is the part of water cycle.

Rain is good rinser,
Rain is natural shower,
Rain is crops grower,
Rain is water recharger.

Education Journey

Modern education Journey starts with
Formal education
Primary education meant for
Literacy mission
Secondary education meant for
Skill generation
Higher secondary education for
Skill cultivation
College education for
Subject specialization
University education for
Ideas contribution.

What actually matters,
how it functions .
Devoted education necessary for
Socio-economic revolution.

To bring growth and development for
any Nation.
Students and teacher must work for
Quality education.

History combine Past Present and Future

We inherit past in the present,
Present deeds shine in the future.

Present is not just present,
As it is built upon our past,
Past is not just dead past.
As it exists in our culture.

History decipher Past in the Present,
To establish truth and take lesson.
It project future on the basis of present.
History is the discipline which unfold Past
To take lesson from the knowledge vast.

India – Economic challenge

For our own country, let me make a brief,
about the problems and everlasting grief,
Poverty and unemployment, it's twin disease,
Socio-religious tensions are still at the crease.

Social weakness and slow economic progress,
for a long time,fail to make planning a success.
There is the condition of social exclusion,
Marginalization and political discrimination.

Till now, equality, freedom and justice is a far cry.
To remove such condition is today's outcry.
There is need to share the fruits of development,
and understanding the under employment.

Law of Nature

Time passes, it never stay,
When a man passes away,
Some people carried away,
Others mostly shy away.
Some people's name stay,
Others name fade away.

Human body die but not it's soul,
Human body vanishes but karma remain,
Soul take birth again and again,
New life is determined by evil or good soul.

Man die but memories never die,
Life is sensable,when memory untie.

Earth Day

Celebrate Earth day
Today and Every day
Take oath to conserve mother earth
And protecting environment.

An appeal to Go green
Every young and teen
Hold mind in high esteem
Work and cooperate in team.

Happy birthday
No party no cake
For God sake!
As our lives are at stake
Due to carona outbreak.

Indian Marriage

Marriage is our old custom,
It is a part of our social system,
It has created the family institution,
It brings two family in close relation.

Marriages are made in heaven,
It binds two odd souls as even.
Man proposes and God disposes
lifelong tie, a marriage presupposes.

Excursion of God

No body has ever seen God
But everybody has seen nature
It's evolution and it's enumerous creatures
They embraced the boon of the nature
As well as taste the wrath of the Nature
All are manifestation of supreme God.

How many people Wish to
Go for excursion of God?
Except for few curious soul,
All wouldn't give their nod !

Today most of the people's belief is-
Every thing is made of tiny particles of matter.
For them, what matters is;
Nothing but worldly transient pleasure!

Understanding of History and Historical writing : (Microscopic view of History)

History is the story of the past.
It's not just the story of the past
It's actually the study of the past
It's infact systematic study of facts of the past
It's precisely the study of historical facts
It mainly concern with the study of significant facts
Historical facts are not only objective facts
These are also subjective facts
These are the construction of individuals.
These includes contemporary writings
Apart from later period writings
History has been written again and again
For the sake of writing improved or better history
Discovery of new and accessibility of facts
Gives new insights to historians
They test to accept and reject facts
Hence facts are not ultimate truth
These are distructible and refutable facts
All historical accounts are contemporary writings
These are products of different space and time.

Multinational Coorporation Role of MNC's:

Oh! Multinational Coorporation.
What a miraculous operation!
With our full cooperation.
Doing admirable function!
Have taken so many actions.

MNC's are acting as a role model,
Their place in the economy is nodal,
They've brought coke and mineral water bottle,
Their technologies are actually latest,
They claim them as the best.

MNC'S produce their products globally,
They make consume these globally.

They're employing cheap labour!
Our government provides them all favour,
They get handsome profit from their endeavour.

MNC'S are spreading consumerism,
The profit is central to capitalism,
They are working as organised vandalism,
They are against the idea of egalitarianism,
Society is at the verge of schism.

Indian Economy

Direction of new economic policy: An impression

Indian industries are not worthless,
But our government is helpless,
Need is to create a goodwill,
By supressing our social ill will.

Lukewarm Indian government has no political will,
In recent years, government is climbing uphill,
It's surprising why government overlook foothill,
Will the government will take the path of downhill?

It's interesting to know whether
India has own economic policy!
After the adoption of globalisation policy,
Our country has lost her independent policy.
What is the need of becoming a part of
Global economy and global consumers,
Parallel to the Indian economy and it's consumers.

There is just creation of affluent middle class,
Which is actually behaving like a sponge,
Shamelessly absorb all the benefits,
To be squeezed for the advancement of their life.
It's good for the growth of world economy,
But for the millions of educated class it's gloomy,
Why this neglect by the democratic government?
A good government works for everyone's betterment.

Directionless Indian Economy

India is a very big country
This is a point to worry
Some groups are developing entirely
Others are rather struggling severely
Is this is the way of protecting democracy
Why some groups are crazy and frenzy?
What's wrong with the Constitution based policy
Political independence is just proving deceiving democracy.

Who is creating gulf in the society
Whether it will lead to social amity
When our country is still developing
Why a small section is prospering
Why the majority of people have no stake
Why this section has no share and cake
Our democracy will be called a fake
Perpetuating socio- economic inequality will be our mistake.

As there is no prospect for the removal of unemployment,
People will give up respect to their leaders and government.

Society at the crossroad

Fir thousands of years,
Indian society had not seen change .
There were more instances of
Continuity than change.

Foreigners came and rule this country,
But failed to change it's culture and society.
Reformers worked to save the identity of,
Indian culture and society.

After independence, the country moved on,
for development and modernization.
The makers of modern India,
Followed the path of Industrialization and Globalization.

As a result India has become,
Neither a traditional nor a Modern society.
India is still a developing economy.
As not achieved the status of a developed economy.

Urbanization drive has given rise to,
A sophisticated cosmopolitan culture.
Aping the Western culture and society,
Has become a common feature of Indian society.

The economic power of a Multinational
Has overpowered the swadesi enterprises or National
The efficiency and commercial success of MNC's
Has made their presence in the economy very vital.

Indian enterprises are competing with MNC's
Some have become swadesi Multinationals
Many others are perishing or dying
That is due to their smallness or being National.

There are the rise of new socio-economic classes
One, with the high purchasing power
Second, with the low purchasing power
Third, with no purchasing power.

In the age of high expectation and consumerism
The country is fulfilling the dreams of a few
Majority of the people are silent viewers
It means that our country is in the hands of a few.

Democracy works at the will of Majority
But minority is not able to fix the country's priority.
As a legacy of the rule of the minority in the country
They wish to keep intact their supremacy.

We have followed the idea of Democracy
In reality our society has become undemocratic
After the 75 years of democratic rule
Why we feel sad and ridicule.

The victory of new social life

India is no more the vanguard of Western Civilization
Slowly slowly it succumb to Western Civilization
It protect her identity for centuries under the foreign rule
Ironically it has started changing under the self rule

Economic issues have become it's main concern
But adopted the morals of modern civilizatiion inturn
There is sign of the breaking of society and family
It has given rise the life of separation and isolation finally

It ended the tradition of community and joint family life
Desire for affluent life forced us to adopt individual life
The traumatic life of parents have no heeling
The emotional feeling has given way to realistic feeling.

Friendship

We come across so many people
In our modern life
Most of them are passerby
And some are nice Guys

We make friendship
With a few of those Guys
We enjoy their company
Only few are so lucky

Friendship needs a test
Those who passes are the best
A friend in deed
Is friend indeed!

Friends are a part of
our happiness
They also become support
In time of trouble and sadness

Always talk with good friends
To make them true friends
There are no substitutes of friends
They are medicament of all types of strains.

Chapter – III

My Political Thought

I always wish to spread the fragrance of humanity: An Introspection

I always,
Wish to spread
the fragrance of humanism,
in my vicinity
and beyond,
in all over the world.

In Reality,
Humanism
is the supreme religion
on the earth,
that can become
Saviour of decaying
human civilization,
restoring that only worth.

I feel,
Our prime minister
Narendra Modijee,

is the epitome
of humanism,
Who is working
for fulfilling,
the needs and desire
of millions of people,
Who are hoping
to rebuild
a just and
"Dignified" society,
in the whole world.

I am hopeful,
that the spirit of
Humanism will engulf
many of us,
at the time of
severe 'crisis'
to repeal any type of
dangerous threat
over the peaceful
Citizens of the world.

Ram Mohan Roy

Ram Mohan Roy was the father of modern India,
As he laid the foundation of many pioneering Idea.
Became the leading social crusader;
Projected as an ardent religious reformer,
Credited with ban on sati partha
Criticized caste system and Idol worship
Worked for monotheism and attacked rituals
To spread his massage founded Brahmo samaj
Ram Mohan Roy wad the founder of Hindu College
Wished to spread western philosophy and knowledge
Champion of the modern English education
supporter of the freedom of press in India.

Gandhiji: (profession to Politics)

Gandhiji went to South Africa,
on the Dada Abdullah "Aagraha",
Pleaded case for his company,
Fought against injustices to many.
He devised a unique political tool,
named 'Satyagraha' in political school,
It was based on truth and non-violence,
designed to succeed on followers compliance.
He fought against racist British rule,
in the foreign land,
Later, in 1915 he returned to India,
to free his motherland.
He United people of various sections,
to oppose foreign rule and take actions.

He raised various mass movement,
strictly limited to peaceful movement.
He controlled differences,discord and dissention,
to achieve the political goal of national liberation.

Present World Order

Today is time to scrutiny,
The world order.
The world appears to be,
at the verge of great disorder.
The world is not safe for,
a peaceful life .
The world is not pollution free,
poses threat to human life.
The world is confronting with,
Social and economic strife.
Top of all, the world is
Shaken by a virus disease strike.
The most pertinent question is
Who is responsible for such order?

The perplexing matter before us is
to prove ourselves civilized and crusader.
The prudent decision is yet to come,
for a humanitarian efforts to overcome,
unwanted violence and inhuman development,
menace for natural and social environment.

Victory- Final Destination

The victory for humanity,
for the world community,
for a country or the society,
is meaningful and desired,,
Although,in the materialistic world,
it is distant dream and far cry.

The victory in the battleground,
in the modern democratic politics,
and in the realm of ideas,
give chance to many individuals,
to exercise and enhance,
the power to exercise their supremacy.

The victory make many people,
blind haughty and arrogant.
They behave with others,
like a dictator or a tyrant.
Why the victory for some,
make the life of many bothersome?

We need some capable leaders,
to run society and politics,
like a propeller or machine,
to fly a rocket or an aeroplane.
Ready to work tirelessly and with perfection,
like natural law and devine dictation.

Chapter - IV

Stanzas

Meghdoot

Summer is passing soon,
Atmosphere is nearly cool.
It's surely onset of monsoon,
Monsoon rain farmer's boon.

History Timeline:

We inherit the past in the present.
Present deeds shine in the future.
Present is not just present,
As it is built upon our past.
Past is not just dead past,
As it exists in our culture.

Agenda of Swadeshi

We are mindlessly aping the west,
Do you think we are giving our best?

Time has arrived for our real test,
Propagate Swadeshi without any rest.

Save our country from western arrest,
Do something to avoid social unrest .

I Wish

Make the present memorable,
Free of worldly trouble.
Attain progress that is laudable
Think a development which is sustainable

Life

Sometimes life is wonderful,
Sometimes life is woeful,
Sometimes life is wishful,
Sometimes life is wailful,
Sometimes life is whirlpool,
Sometimes life is wrathful,
Sometimes life is wistful,
Ensure life is wonderful .

Reality

Everybody talk about reality,
No body knows the true reality,
As reality has not a single face,
Actually the reality has many face.

Reality is that which impinge from outside,
It is discovered, when we put "insight".
Reality is fractured when we go inside,
Those who can see all,they have "sight".

Myth

Myth has no teeth,
It lay beneath the truth.
Myth is like truth,
When reality is beneath.

Fact

Facts are really sacred,
Though opinion is free.
Some facts are infallible,
Some facts are destructible.
Some facts are same for all,
Historical facts are specific to all.

Truth

Truth always triumph,
Truth must triumph.
Truth should prevail everywhere,
Truth has moral Power.
Truth clean our soul,
Truth is beautiful.
Always speak truth,
Work for truth.
Live a truthful life,
Only truth will remain alive.

Hope

Hope is possible,
It is expectation,
To hope is universal,
It is but natural.

Hope is a positive,
and constructive thought.
It can be fulfilled,
One must sought.

Hope is life
No life without hope
Hope is like clouds
Some passes by some gives rain.

Time

Time and tides,waits
for none.
Time is money,if lost
never come.
Time is ever-changing
in the form of
Cyclic or linear.
It is progressively moving,
from antiquity
to present year.
Sometimes it repeats,
A silver lining!
Mostly it mends,
which is preceding.

3×10

One, Two , Three,
VI want to break free.
Four, Five, Six,
Everything is infix.
Seven, Eight, Nine,
All are feeling fine.
Ten, Eleven,Twelve,
We lack safety valve.
Thirteen,Fourteen,Fifteen
Great kings and queen.
Sixteen, Seventeen, Sixteen,
Almighty God,who has seen.

Nineteen,Twenty,Twenty-one,
Freedom and Justice to everyone.
Twenty-two,Twenty-three,Twenty-four,
Experiences are sweet and sour.
Twenty-five,Twenty-six,Twenty-seven,
Marriages are built in the heaven.
Twenty-eight, Twenty-nine,Thirty
Small towns are mostly dirty.

The Arrow

The archers bow and arrow,
Not to hit a cuckoo or a crow.
The tragedy is loss of sparrow!
None can trace sign of sorrow.

Law of piety we must borrow,
Let love and compassion grow.
Never our thinking be narrow,
Happy days will come tomorrow.

My Hobby

Some students are dull in study
As well as 'sans' any hobby.

Some students are not good in study
Yet they cultivate some hobby.

Some students are serious in study
But they don't have any hobby.

Some students enjoy study with some hobby
Games,drawing,painting are popular hobby

A Man

A man when,
he is growing,
Spend his time,
in knowing!
A man when,
he is thoughtful,
Try to know
Everything doubtful.
A man when
He is working,
Remain sincere and honest
For good earning .
A man when
He is retired,
Take rest and become careful,
To enjoy what he acquired.

A Boy

A boy with toy
Play all time with joy
A boy with no toy
Looks dull and shy.

Naughty boy

You naughty boy,
Looking all the time toy.
You want to try,
Failing everytime makes you cry.
Carelessly makes everything destroy,
You are then filled with joy.
At once you run and fly
You fear to give any reply.

Santa Clause

On the Christmas day night,
O dear Santa clause!
At the midst of twinkling lights,
All children,welcome you with applause!

As You love,we little children,
land on Earth to join our happiness,
Sing and play to become wild,
Thanks to your colourful dress,sweets and all goodness.

God

Oh god ! You are great !
You have power to create,
and destroy everything.
I pray for your kindness,
and blessings,
so that I can do many things.

Life

Life is struggle and struggle is life,
In every sphere of life we see struggle,
as it is always present in the
individual, social economic or political life,

We shall not give up struggle in our life,
Life of great men always remained in struggle,
Their life still stands inspiring for us,
So struggle,to keep alive struggle,in our life.

Sometimes

Sometimes life is tuff,
Sometimes life is easy,
Sometimes life is dull,
Sometimes life is busy.

Life is often miserable,
When wife is intolerable.
Life is cumbersome,
When salary is not handsome.

Modern life is full of strife,
But still we admire and like,
Even face all hardships that strike.
Winning all hurdles,we feel Pride.

Ting Tong Rhymes

Ting tong,sing a song ,
Ding dong,watch a song,
Ping pong,play a song,
King Kong,listen a song.

Bing Bang,Atom bomb,
Zig zag,tyrant comb,
Dig dung,future womb,
MIG mango,human tomb.

Fringe afar,bright light,
Singe star,light slight,
Ringe Sagar,pearl bright,
Striking sitar,soul height.

A Dreamer

I am a fantastic dreamer,
Often travel in dream steamer,
Dream is like a burner,
Give me a chance to be a dreamer.

Though not to be a big dreamer,
I want to be a humble learner,
Let live simple living but think higher,
Sometimes Sword,Sometimes Pen make us mightier.

Great man is always called a dreamer
He even prove himself a practitioner.
Great man always stood for a reason
Because he has a vision.

Position of Star

A natural Star is very far,
A religious Star is very far,
A film Star is very far,
A sports Star is very far,
A political Star is very far,
An academic Star is very far,
They are very far,but still Star,
Their position in society is HIGH like ALTAR
The stars are very popular
Theirs performance are spectacular
Everybody wants to become a star
Only a few becomes real star.

Time (2)

Once upon a time,
Life of man Become fine,
Everything was savage and prestine.

Time comes and go,
Once gone, never return,
Become alert! for it's new turn.

Time is moving on and on,
It never stop and never say no,
Time never become tired, one must know.

Alice in wonderland

Don't aspire to be an Alice in Wonderland,
Make Wonderland to our motherland,
Let's walk hand in hand,
Journey may be small but make it grand.

Life is not worthless,
Although not always sweet,
Life may be sour and spiceless,
Learn to make it yummy and tweet.

The cradle of memory,
An inward inquiry,
Sometimes gloomy,
Sometimes happy.

Karma

Karma is a deed which determines
The fate of a person.
Karma is of two types;
Good and bad.
Karma is the nature of our actions,
As our actions are either good or bad.

Man live in a society and makes
Their own law.
Man sometimes also breaks
Some laws
Time to time man has to
Test their law.

Karma is our worship
Karma pays in our hardship .

There is...

There is a rat
Sitting on a mat
Looking very fat
Eating this that.

There is a lovely ground
Walk inside and move around
Observe players in your surround
Runners daily running here several round

There is a snowy Mountain
It has beautiful hot water fountain
Attracts us again and again
Enjoy Nature on the Toy Train.

There is vast resources
But relatively less opportunities
Where there is a will
There is a way.

Chapter – V

Haikus

Monsoon

In the rainy season sun often lost in the clouds,
Play hide and seek game with the clouds,
Form rainbow as sunlight fall on suspended water drops

When the clouds are laden with water droplets,
Water downpour like a natural shower for hours,
When rain stops,sky smile with rainbow colours.

Monsoon rain often late, sometimes, on time,
On it's arrival, Indian farmers feel well and fine,
Bumper harvest, makes country safe and shine.

Society

Literature is the mirror of a society,
Image is not monolithic but appears in variety,
Stereotypes and prejudice hide overall truth of a society.,

Nature and signature never change
Development change the nature of a society
Change for the better should be our priority.

The voice of the wise
Make many surprise
Even though meant for retrieve.

Modern society

Modern society is progressing,
Though,civilization is regressing.
Achievements,but not without a price.

Ofcourse,there is development of modern science and technology,
Although, it has led to the concentration of wealth and it's eulogy.
Worse is the sufferings of millions,who live in socio-economic strife.

"Education for all",
"Work for all",
Makes a country tall.

Time - 1

Time comes and go,
everyone shall take some vow,
do some great and memorable show.

Time is precious,it is a fact
Time passes but the saying is still intact
Canonical words are often correct.

Time and tides waits for none
Make sure that your all important work done
The dictum must be followed by everyone.

Man

Man life is for name and fame
Man's life is not for insane and shame
Man's life is not a curse or a game

Man's life is to tame nature,
and put in the human frame.
Not to defame and blame God.

Let's live in band
And walk hand in hand
Lest we don't fall on sand.

Nature

Small is beautiful
The few is weak and bold
All that glitters are not gold.

Birds of a feather flock together
Like minded people co-operate and greet each other
Country men must live unitedly and work together.

Future can't be good, if our resources are deminishing,
Future can be safe if we don't do any mistake and waste
Future could be vibrant if the nature is not tyrant.

Worldly Life

World is the stage of a big drama,
God raise the curtain of all "characters",
Some are seen as vector and some are as nectar.

Weather changes, life changes,
Time transform our thinking,
Whereas,money shapes our lifestyle.

World is full of battle and wars,
World is full of mistries and scars,
World is full of legends and Stars.

Platform

Platform is where train arrives and make departure,
Platform is where aeroplane land and fly,
Platform is the launching pad for our career.

Resources
Resources on Earth is bountiful,
But lives of many is still pitiful,
Sufferings of man is very shameful.

Nature
Nature may be wrathful,
Nature may be blissful,
Live friendly and make it joyful.

Environment

Inside a forest, everything is not at rest,
Site of several life struggle and to prove their best,
Survival of those,who passes the test.

A season come and go
Birds flock together and migrate
Nature make this certain every year.

Sun rises in the East,
Sun sets in the west,
One cannot change this,try your best.

Mountains

Mountains have lofty peaks and narrow valleys,
Sea has high tides and low tides,
Similarly, human life has ups and downs.

Mountains are high and standing as physical barrier,
Mountain Passes make the movement of people easier,
These passes acts as "goods" and culture carrier.

Mountains grow several dry fruits and medicinal herbs,
Mountains provide fresh water and hygienic weather,
It's beautiful nature has given us several hill stations.

Conservation of Nature

Mountains are high and covered with trees and bushes,
Mountains are source of many springs and sacred rivers,
Mountains were shelter for hermit and sages.

Making good friendship is important,
To become environment friendly is more important,
Fixing our priority is even more important.

Nature cares all of us,
It has provided beautiful things,
Nature expects our caring hands.

Nature and Man

Mamooth to miniature,
Nature has created all the creatures,
As friends,as foes they live together.

Man has developed a distinct speech,
Man has developed a complex brain,
Man has able to discover and invent again and again.

In den ,Lion takes rest,
Birds lives in their Nest,
Human houses are the best.

Manifestation of Nature

Nature often becomes furious,
Make man to remain curious,
Don't take it easy,be serious.

In summer,Sun glare like flame,
In raining season,sun play hide and seek game
In winter,we relish bright sunshine.

Tiny and shiny Dew drops of winter morning,
Spread over grasses and leaves of plants,
Easily visible as we rub our window pan.

The world at our hands

The sky is full of tiny twinkling stars,
Atmosphere is full of useful and harmful gases,
Earth is full of natural and man-made objects.

The world is full of hope and despair,
World is full of tragedy,comedy and demogogy,
World is full joy,prosperity and philanthropy.

Green Earth,clean Earth,
Green Nature,Dream Nature,
Go Green,Glow Dream.

Time (2)

Once upon a time,
Life of man Become fine,
Everything was savage and prestine.

Time comes and go,
Once gone, never return,
Become alert! for it's new turn.

Time is moving on and on,
It never stop and never say no,
Time never become tired,one must know.

Reflection of society

Many people lives in a society
In many ways, they are similar,
In some ways they are also disimilar.

Politics revolves around 'Power ',
Leaders bothers about 'followers'.
People looks for their actual 'well-wishers'.

Society has influence over individuals,
Some great individuals can influence society,
Sometimes a society is either status quoist or open minded.